I am Harry Houdini

adapted by Brooke Vitale

PENGUIN YOUNG READERS LICENSES
An Imprint of Penguin Random House LLC, New York

© and TM 9 Story Media Group Inc. All rights reserved.

Published in 2020 by Penguin Young Readers Licenses, an imprint of Penguin Random House LLC, New York. Manufactured in China.

Visit us online at www.penguinrandomhouse.com.

ISBN 9780593096383   10 9 8 7 6 5 4 3 2 1

Xavier sighed happily. "Ah, there's nothing like camping out under the stars with your Nature Troop and best friends," he said.

Brad grinned. They were spending the night in the museum's nature exhibit. "My first full night in the museum," he said quietly. "I'm so excited."

Beside him, Yadina yawned and closed her eyes. Xavier quickly fell asleep, too. Soon, only Brad was still awake.

He looked around at the stars filling the sky. Through the museum's speakers, he heard owls hooting and crickets chirping.

It wasn't long before Brad's excitement turned to worry. He nervously pulled his sleeping bag up to his chin. He loved this exhibit, but he had never noticed how *spooky* it was.

Suddenly, he saw a large, scary shadow in the corner of the room. "*Ahh!* Ghost!"

Brad jumped out of his sleeping bag and raced for the door. He pushed against it as hard as he could, but it wouldn't move. He was stuck!

"You have to pull," Yadina said, joining him at the door.

Xavier rubbed his eyes. "You okay, Brad?"

Brad shook his head. "I don't think I can stay in the museum all night," he said. "I mean, I want to, but it's way too scary."

"Hmm, this sounds like a big problem," Xavier said. "Are you thinking what I'm thinking?" he asked Yadina.

Yadina nodded. "To the Secret Museum!"

Pulling open the door, the friends tiptoed through the museum. Slowly, they made their way through the dark hallways to the Secret Museum. Inside, they found a key sitting on a podium.

"A key? I wonder what it opens," Yadina said.

"Maybe the front door!" Brad said. "I guess the Secret Museum agrees. It's too scary here. I'll just let myself out."

Brad picked up the key. He was headed for the exit when a hologram appeared.

"Look! The museum doesn't want you to go," Xavier called. "It wants you to meet Harry Houdini."

Sighing, Brad turned back to the podium. "How can Harry Houdini help me get through a whole night in the museum? Do you think he has ghost repellent?"

"Only one way to find out," Xavier answered. "Ready for adventure?"

With a great flash of light, the friends were sent back to Wisconsin in 1881.

In a nearby field, they saw a tent.

"A circus!" Yadina shouted.

"Cool," Xavier said. "But why would the museum send us to a circus?"

Brad grinned. "Because circuses are fun and not scary at all?"

Just then, a twig cracked in the bushes behind the friends. The branches rustled, and a young boy appeared.

Brad screamed, terrified.

"Oh! Sorry about that," the boy said. "My mom says I'm always surprising people. Try taking a deep breath to calm down. It will make you feel better."

While Brad tried to catch his breath, Xavier looked at the boy. "It's him. It's Harry Houdini," he whispered.

"Are you going to the circus, too?" Harry asked.

Yadina grinned. "We are now!"

Harry and the friends made their way to the tent. Peeking inside, they saw a man standing at the top of a high platform. Across from him was another high platform. A thin wire stretched between the two.

"It's him," Harry whispered, taking a poster out of his pocket. "Fearless Jean."

Brad watched in awe as Fearless Jean put one foot on the wire. "He's not going to walk across that . . . is he?"

No one answered. They were all too busy watching.

"Wow!" Harry said as Jean made his way, step by step, across the wire.

"Talk about brave!" Xavier added.

High up on the wire, Jean paused and took a deep breath. Then he began to balance on one foot!

"That's what I want to do one day," Harry said. "Be a brave performer and amaze people."

"You do?" Brad asked, shocked. "But being a brave performer looks scary."

Harry nodded. "Maybe a little. But I *really* want to try, even if I'm nervous. So I'd better start practicing!" he said. "Will you help me?"

The friends found themselves outside Harry's house. They nervously watched as he tried to walk across a thin beam on the ground.

"You can do it!" Yadina shouted.

Harry held out his arms and lifted one foot. "*Whooooa!*" he shouted. Wobbling, he fell off the beam.

"Maybe we should try something a little easier first," Xavier suggested.

Harry nodded. Laying a piece of rope on the ground, he practiced walking across that. Xavier and Yadina crossed behind him.

"Brad, are you coming?" Yadina asked.

Brad put one foot on the rope. Then the next. "Now this I can handle!" he said, grinning.

"Okay," Harry said. "I'm ready. It's time to raise the rope."

Harry bent down to gather the rope. But as he picked it up, his hands and feet got caught!

The more Harry tried to free himself, the more tangled he got. Finally, he stopped moving and took a deep breath. Then, slowly, he slipped free of the rope.

"How did you do that?" Brad asked.

"I just took a deep, calming breath," Harry said. "It helps me get out of tight spots, and makes me feel better."

Xavier took one side of the rope. "Maybe you should work that into your circus act," he said, tying the rope to a tree.

"Maybe," Harry said. "But is escaping from being tied up exciting?"

Finally, the rope was ready for Harry's next attempt. He climbed up and took one step. Then he began to wobble. Holding out his arms, he steadied himself. But as he tried to take another step, he fell off the rope.

"I'm too nervous," he said. "But Fearless Jean wasn't."

"I wonder how he stayed so calm when he was doing something so scary," Xavier said.

Harry thought back to Fearless Jean's act. "Just before he did his trick, he took a big deep breath. That must be it! He took deep breaths to calm down, just like I did when I was tangled in the rope!"

Harry took a deep breath and stepped back onto the rope. "I'm ready to try again!"

As the friends watched, Harry took one step. Then another. And another. Finally, he made it to the other side of the rope!

"Wow!" Brad said, watching Harry. "I wonder if taking a deep breath to calm down will actually help him become a brave performer like Fearless Jean."

At that moment, Berby appeared.

"Looks like we're about to find out," Xavier said.

The friends took hold of Berby. There was a bright flash, and the sound of applause filled the air.

Brad pointed at a stage, where a grown-up Harry stood, bowing to a happy audience.

"He really did become a brave performer, just like he wanted!" Brad said. "So, maybe I can spend the night in the museum . . . or at least try to."

Yadina smiled. "I know you can, Brad."

Xavier nodded. "Let's go home!"

The friends reached out for Berby again. A moment later, they were back in the museum.

"Okay, here we go," Brad said. "Spending the whole night in the museum. The dark museum."

As they walked back toward the nature exhibit, Brad spotted a dark, scary shadow. "Oh no! It's . . . it's . . ."

"Remember, take a deep breath, like Harry Houdini taught us," Xavier said.

Brad nodded and took a deep breath. Then he walked up to the shadow. "Hey, it's just Murray!" he said, looking up at the museum's *T. rex* skeleton. "I see him every day. You're not scary, Murray."

Feeling better, Brad confidently went back to the nature exhibit.

"You know, you guys were right," Brad said, sliding into his sleeping bag. "The museum really is neat at night. But . . . you're still going to stay close by, right?"

Yadina and Xavier each reached out and took one of Brad's hands. "Right."

Brad smiled. "Good night, Yadina. Good night, Xavier. Good night, Murray."

As Brad closed his eyes, a creepy voice came back to him. It was Yadina, pretending to be Murray. "Good *niiiight*, Brad!"